W9-BHG-497

SHEEP

BY MARV ALINAS

PUBLISHED BY THE CHILD'S WORLD®

Published by The Child's World®
1980 Lookout Drive • Mankato, MN 56003-1705
800-599-READ • www.childsworld.com

ACKNOWLEDGMENTS
The Child's World®: Mary Swensen, Publishing Director
The Design Lab: Design
Michael Miller: Editing
Sarah M. Miller: Editing

DESIGN ELEMENTS
© Doremi/Shutterstock.com

PHOTO CREDITS
© 5PH/Shutterstock.com: 16; Apichart Patana-anek/Shutterstock.
com: 8-9; Baronb/Shutterstock.com: cover; Budimir Jevtic/
Shutterstock.com: 6; Heath Johnson/Shutterstock.com: 20-21; Mats/
Shutterstock.com: 19; Paul Looyen/Shutterstock.com: 12; Repina
Valeriya/Shutterstock.com: 15; TFoxFoto/Shutterstock.com: 11;
TOMO/Shutterstock.com: 5; Zbyszko/Shutterstock.com: 10

ISBN: 9781503808300
LCCN: 2015958478

Printed in the United States of America
Mankato, MN
June, 2016
PA02308

Table of Contents

Cute Sheep

"Baa!" A sheep is calling out. Sheep have four legs. They have two toes on each of their four feet. Most sheep are covered in **wool**. A sheep's coat of wool is called its **fleece**.

DID YOU KNOW?

SHEEP WEIGH BETWEEN 88 AND 350 POUNDS
(40 AND 159 KILOGRAMS).

DID YOU KNOW?

THERE ARE ABOUT 900 KINDS OF SHEEP.

Different Colors

Some sheep have a white body and a white face. Others have a black or spotted face. Some sheep are all brown or black.

Farm Life

Many sheep are raised on big farms. Sheep need a lot of room to wander and eat.

DID YOU KNOW?

A GROUP OF SHEEP IS CALLED A HERD, A FLOCK, OR A MOB.

Males and Females

Male sheep are called **rams**.
Rams have horns.

Female sheep are called **ewes** (YOOZ). Ewes produce milk.

DID YOU KNOW?

THE SOUND SHEEP MAKE IS CALLED BLEATING.

Baby Sheep

A baby sheep is called a **lamb**. A lamb drinks its mother's milk until it is about three months old.

Eating

Sheep eat plants. They eat grasses and flowers. Farm sheep often eat dried grass called **hay**.

DID YOU KNOW?

LIKE COWS, SHEEP BURP UP AND RE-CHEW THEIR FOOD.

15

Important Sheep

Sheep are raised for many reasons. Some people eat the meat from sheep. It is called **mutton**.

Sheep also give us milk. It is a bit different from cows' milk. Cheese and yogurt are made from sheep's milk.

Sheep's wool is very important. Cutting the wool is called **shearing**. It does not hurt the sheep.

Wool is used for many things. Clothing and blankets are made from wool.

DID YOU KNOW?

THERE ARE MORE THAN 1 BILLION SHEEP IN THE WORLD.

CHINA HAS THE MOST SHEEP.

DID YOU KNOW?

SHEEP CAN EAT BETWEEN 2 AND 4 POUNDS (1 AND 2 KILOGRAMS) OF FOOD EACH DAY.

Sheep are very important animals. They give many things to people.

Glossary

EWES (YOOZ) Ewes are female sheep.

FLEECE (FLEESS) A sheep's wooly coat is its fleece.

HAY (HAY) Hay is dried grass that is fed to farm animals.

LAMB (LAM) A lamb is a baby sheep.

MUTTON (MUT-tun) Mutton is the meat from sheep.

RAMS (RAMZ) Rams are male sheep.

SHEARING (SHEER-ing) Cutting a sheep's wool is called shearing.

WOOL (WULL) Wool is the thick, curly hair on a sheep.

To Learn More

IN THE LIBRARY

Komiya, Teruyuki. *Life-Size Farm*. New York, NY:
Seven Footer Kids, 2012.

Minden, Cecilia. *Farm Animals: Sheep*. Ann Arbor, MI:
Cherry Lake Publishing, 2013.

Nomad Press. *Wool*. White River Junction, VT:
Nomad Press, 2011.

ON THE WEB

Visit our Web site for links about sheep:
childsworld.com/links

Note to Parents, Teachers, and Librarians: We routinely verify our Web links to make sure
they are safe and active sites. So encourage your readers to check them out!

Index

ABOUT THE AUTHOR

Marv Alinas has lived in Minnesota all her life. When she's not reading or writing, Marv enjoys spending time with her husband and dogs and traveling to interesting places.